Mr Rabbit the Farmer

Story retold by Pauline Chandler
Pictures by Eric Smith

OXFORD
UNIVERSITY PRESS

Every day Mr Rabbit
strolled past Mr Bear's field
and admired the crops.

Mr Bear always grew plenty of fine
fruit and vegetables. He grew marrows
and melons, parsnips and peas. He grew
swedes and strawberries, carrots and
cabbages. Mr Bear's land had such rich
soil that everything he planted grew
very well, and he harvested so much
food that sometimes he had to
throw some away.

Although Mr Bear often had too many crops, he never offered them to his neighbour, Mr Rabbit, who was poor and had no good soil of his own in which to grow food.

While Mr Bear and his family had more than enough to eat, Mr Rabbit and his family often went hungry.

3

"What's for tea?" said the little Rabbits. "What's for tea?"

"Only one old carrot," said Mrs Rabbit.

Mr Rabbit cut up the carrot into equal pieces and handed it out.

"Not one old carrot again!" said the little Rabbits. "We hate those old carrots!"

"That's all we have!" said Mrs Rabbit.

4

Mr Rabbit stood at the fence and looked at Mr Bear's flourishing vegetable crop.

"I wish I had some of this land. I could grow anything then," he muttered. "I could grow cabbages, barley, beans. More cabbages. Anything."

Then Mr Rabbit went back to his own stony patch of land and kicked at the prickly thistles.

"This is the only crop I can grow!" he said.

One day, Mr Bear heard Mr Rabbit complaining and said,

"Mr Rabbit, I have an idea. You could borrow my field."

"Borrow it?"

"Yes. There's no need to pay me for it. You could borrow the field and all I ask in return is that you share the crops with me at harvest time."

6

Mr Rabbit, who knew how to talk to a businessman, stood deep in thought. Then he scratched his chin and said,

"Share the crop? So we take half each?"

"Yes. I'll take the tops and you take the bottoms," said Mr Bear.

"You take the tops?"

"Yes."

"And I take the bottoms?"

"Yes."

"Done. We have a deal!" said Mr Rabbit, shaking paws.

But as Mr Rabbit watched Mr Bear lope away, he noticed him chuckle.

So, there was a trick in it somewhere.

Mr Bear laughed and laughed all the way home. What a bargain! Mr Rabbit would do all the work, but he, Mr Bear, would take the tops of the plants and leave Mr Rabbit the bottoms. And what good were the bottoms? No good at all. Mr Bear laughed and laughed.

9

All spring and summer Mr Rabbit worked hard on the land. He planted the seeds, pulled up the weeds, and watched his crop ripen in the long sunny days. Then it was time for the harvest.

Mr Rabbit sent a message to Mr Bear.

Dear Mr Bear,
It's time to harvest the crops. Come and collect your tops.
From
Mr Rabbit

So Mr Bear called his family together, gave each of them a wheelbarrow, and led them down to the field, where Mr Rabbit and his family stood waiting.

"Thanks for coming so quickly," said Mr Rabbit. "We can't lift our bottoms until you take your tops."

And he stood back to show Mr Bear a splendid field full of carrots.

But Mr Bear had shaken paws, so he had to take all the tops, the green leaves and stalks, and let Mr Rabbit have all the bottoms, the juicy carrots!

13

When it was time to plant the field again, Mr Rabbit went to see his neighbour, Mr Bear.

"Could I borrow your field?" he said.

"Yes, but this time, I'll take the bottoms and you take the tops," said Mr Bear.

"You take the bottoms?"

"Yes."

"And I take the tops?"

"Yes."

"Done. We have a deal!"
said Mr Rabbit, shaking paws.
Mr Bear smiled at him. "You'll not
trick me twice," he said to himself.
And Mr Rabbit smiled back and
thought, "Don't be so sure."

Mr Rabbit set to work on the field. He planted the seeds, pulled up the weeds, and watched his crop ripen in the long sunny days. Then it was time for the harvest.

Mr Rabbit sent a message to Mr Bear.

Dear Mr Bear,
It's time to harvest the crops. Come and collect your bottoms.
From
Mr Rabbit

So Mr Bear called his family together and led them down to the field, where Mr Rabbit and his family stood waiting.

When it was time to plant the field again, Mr Rabbit went to see Mr Bear.

"Could I borrow your field?" he said.

Mr Bear had his answer ready. "Yes, but this time, I'll take both the tops and the bottoms. You take the middles."

"You take the tops and the bottoms?"

"Yes."

"The tops?"

"Yes."

"**And** the bottoms?"

"Yes."

"And I take the **middles**?"

"YES!"

18

"Done. We have a deal,"
said Mr Rabbit, shaking paws.
And Mr Bear smiled at him.
"You won't trick me this
time!" he said to himself.
And Mr Rabbit smiled
back and thought, "Oh yes,
I will!"

Mr Rabbit set to work on the field. He planted the seeds, pulled up the weeds, and watched his crop ripen in the long sunny days. And when it was time for the harvest, Mr Rabbit sent a message to Mr Bear.

Dear Mr Bear,
It's time to harvest the crops. Come and collect your tops and bottoms.
From
Mr Rabbit

Mr Bear called his family together and led them to the field, where Mr Rabbit and his family stood waiting with handcarts.

As Mr Bear came close to the field, he saw Mr Rabbit and his family standing in front of a towering crop of sweetcorn. But then he saw that the corn cobs, which grow in the middle of the stalks, had all gone. Only the feathery tops and the roots were left.

"I've taken the middles!" shouted Mr Rabbit, at the same time giving a signal to his wife.

There was the rumble of cartwheels as she and his family began to carry home a magnificent crop of corn. "We've left you the tops and the bottoms!"